Why Do Camels Spit?

BY JERYL CHRISTMAS

THIS BOOK BELONGS TO

This book is dedicated to my inquisitive
grandchildren, Elise and Jackson,
and grandnephews, Tate and Parks.

To question is to learn.

Why do camels spit and donkeys kick
whenever they want to?

Why are tigers bold and pandas shy
when living in a zoo?

Why do bunnies hop and spiders crawl
when moving place to place?

Why are cheetahs fast and sloths so slow
in setting their own pace?

Why do boas squeeze and peacocks spread
their feathers open wide?

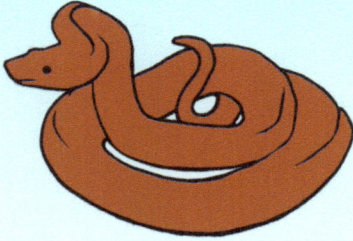

Why are hippos huge and fleas so small
they must be magnified?

Why do hyenas laugh and gray wolves howl
while on the desert plain?

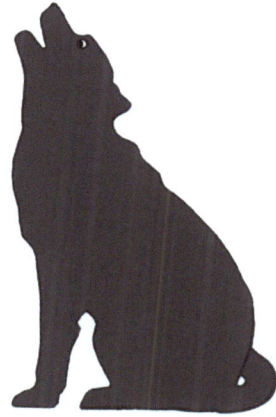

Why are longhorn sheep and mountain goats
so skilled on rough terrain?

Why do kittens purr and cattle moo
when everything's all right?

Why are zebra stripes and stinky skunks
completely black and white?

Why do lions roar and piglets snort
to make their voices heard?

Why are ostriches and emus
not like any other bird?

Why do chickens cluck and loud geese honk
when things don't go their way?

Why are bear cubs and their siblings
always in the mood to play?

Why do panthers prowl and ponies prance
when moving all about?

Why are aardvarks and some monkeys
both endowed with that huge snout?

Why do possums freeze and lizards lose
their tails when danger's near?

Why are rabbits and small field mice
always quivering in fear?

Why do squids squirt ink and cobras hiss
to help in their defense?

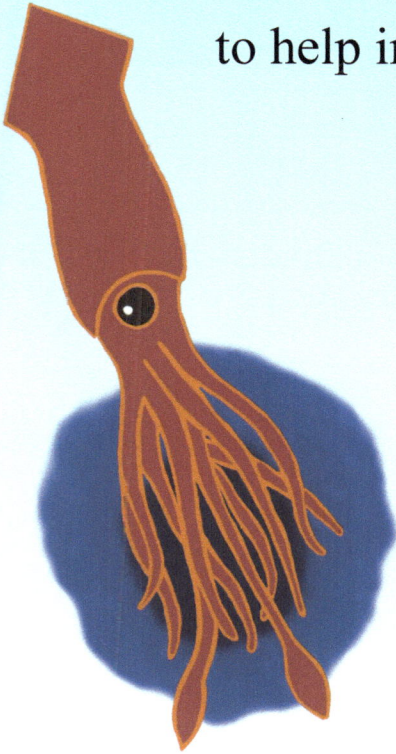

Why are great white sharks and grizzlies
so predaceous and intense?

Why do condors and bald eagles glide
and rarely flap their wings?

Why are jellyfish and bumblebees
both known for their bad stings?

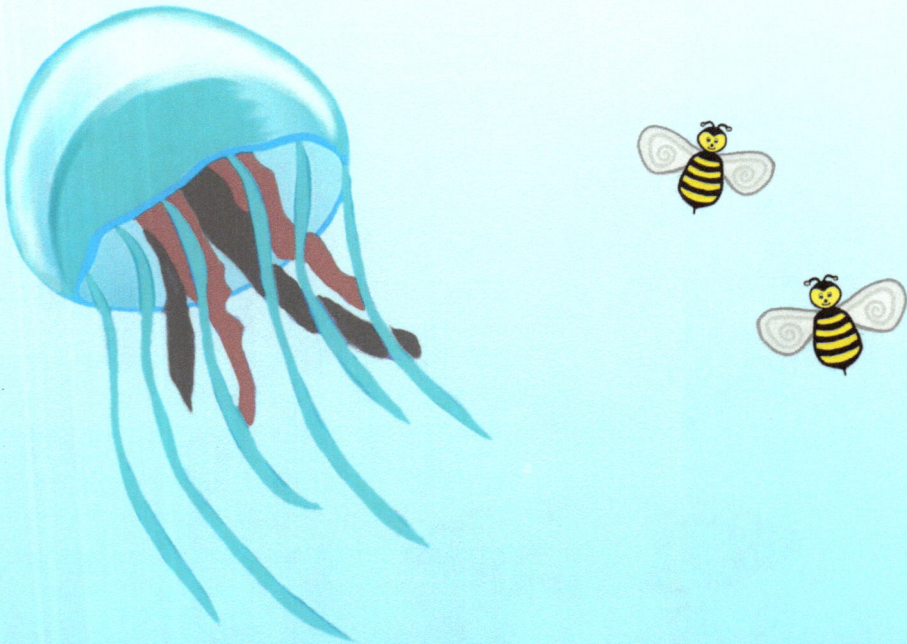

Why do penguins and harp seals prefer
the cold and never freeze?

Why are groundhogs and brown beavers
always chewing on hard trees?

Why do cuckoo birds and bluejays raid
a nest that is not theirs?

Why are mantids' front legs folded
like they're poised for saying prayers?

Why do turtle doves and swans commit
to one long lifetime mate?

Why are some wolves known as alpha males
the ones which dominate?

Why do joeys and koalas live
inside a mother's pouch?

Why are greyhounds outside racing
while a lapdog's on the couch?

Why do myna birds and parrots talk
so humans understand?

Why are gooney birds so graceful
in the air but not on land?

Why do ladybugs and beetles have
six legs instead of eight?

Why are bats equipped with sonar
using sound to navigate?

Why do leopards and dalmations sport
those spots upon their coats?

Why are bullfrogs always croaking
those loud sounds deep in their throats?

Why do geckos and chameleons leave
their babies when they're born?

Why are narwhals and some rhinos
given just that one big horn?

I know God made each creature
in the air, land, and the sea.

He made us all so different.

There is

NO ONE

just like ...

ME!

To question is to learn.

The End